STRONGER THAN YOU KNOW

T0343543

STRONGER THAN YOU KNOW

An Hachette UK Company
www.hachette.co.uk

Vie Books, an imprint of Summersdale Publishers Ltd
Part of Octopus Publishing Group Limited
Carmelite House
50 Victoria Embankment
LONDON
EC4Y 0DZ
UK

www.summersdale.com

Printed and bound in Poland

ISBN: 978-1-80007-341-8

Substantial discounts on bulk quantities of Summersdale books are available to corporations, professional associations and other organizations. For details contact general enquiries: telephone: +44 (0) 1243 771107 or email: enquiries@summersdale.com.

Neither the author nor the publisher can be held responsible for any loss or claim arising out of the use, or misuse, of the suggestions made herein. None of the views or suggestions in this book are intended to replace medical opinion from a doctor. If you have any concerns about your health, please seek professional advice.

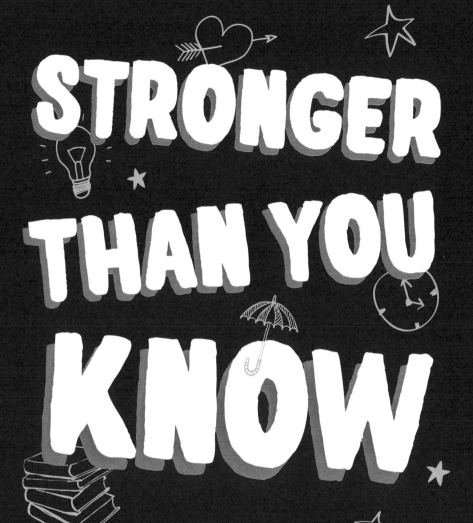

STRONGER THAN YOU KNOW

Find Your Shine and Be Confidently You

POPPY O'NEILL

CONTENTS

119   Part 7:
Be true to yourself

134   Part 8:
Looking forward

FOREWORD

Confidence and resilience are two essential qualities for not only good mental health but for living a positive, fulfilled life. Those of us who are lucky enough to have (or to have learned how to develop) a deep sense of confidence and resilience tend to take this for granted and sometimes find it hard to understand and relate to those for whom this is a daily struggle.

There are so many different factors that can influence our sense of self-confidence and resilience for either better or worse. These include our family, our home environment, school, friendships, exam pressures, relationships, social media, not to mention the health of society and the world at large. Is it any wonder then why so many of us start life thinking there is something wrong with us, putting ourselves down or not feeling able to speak out at different times?

This new book from Poppy O'Neill explores this critical issue of self-confidence in a highly accessible and readable way. My hope is that it will become an instructive workbook to help teenagers and their families understand and work with these issues.

The book starts with an introduction to help readers understand what confidence is, what impacts our self-confidence and there is a helpful guide to show what a high level of confidence feels like. From there, Poppy explores a variety of ways of boosting self-confidence, each of which has solid evidence backing it up. I was particularly struck by the section on being assertive, saying no and getting chatting. While each of these can be very challenging, they can also be very powerful methods for helping us to feel better about ourselves.

I highly recommend this book and hope that it acts as a supportive resource to help teenagers to not only recognize what is causing their self-confidence issues but to build a toolbox of strategies to help them address both the symptoms and the underlying issues.

Graham Kennedy MA, UKCP Reg
Integrative Child & Adolescent Psychotherapist
Attachment and Trauma Consultant

January 2022

INTRODUCTION

Welcome to *Stronger Than You Know*, a guide to growing a healthy sense of self-confidence. When you have high self-confidence, you have faith in yourself and show resilience when faced with new challenges. Building up your self-confidence and learning how to keep it high will serve you well during good times as well as tough ones.

When you're a teen, your brain is changing and growing at an incredible rate. This is brilliant, because it means you're able to learn new skills and take on new information, plus you have bags and bags of creativity and ingenuity. The downside is, you're also more sensitive to negative messages and pressures from the world around you. All the stresses of everyday life can make you feel like you're not good enough and that everyone else is doing better than you.

This book uses a mix of activities, ideas and proven techniques used by therapists – like cognitive behavioural therapy (CBT) and mindfulness – to help you see through the negativity and appreciate yourself for the strong, capable young person you really are. It will help you see yourself and others in a more positive light, act with confidence and live your best life.

IT'S OK NOT TO BE OK

Confidence is weird. Why is it that some people believe in themselves so much more than others? It can seem like everyone else has self-confidence in spades, and you're the only one struggling.

While it may look that way on the outside, the truth is, you're far from the only one. Some people are very good at faking confidence but, deep down, we all doubt ourselves and our abilities sometimes.

It's OK to find things difficult, daunting or downright terrifying. It's OK to need help, reassurance and support. You are just as deserving of patience and understanding as anybody else, and there are people in your life who care about you and want to help you achieve your goals. They want to know when it's hard, when you're feeling stuck or confused and what's on your mind.

You don't have to have everything figured out in order to enjoy life; it's all one big learning curve. The secret is to accept yourself, go at your own pace and remember that it's OK to be exactly as you are right now.

WHAT THIS BOOK WILL DO FOR YOU

This book will help you understand how confidence works, as well as show you how to bring out your own confidence and harness your strength.

The more you learn about your mind, the easier you'll find it to hack confidence and shrink self-doubt down to size. So, if you're fed up of low self-confidence and want to take charge of your emotions, you've come to the right place.

Everything you need to be your strongest, most confident self is already inside you, and this book will help you unlock it. Take a deep breath and remember: you're stronger than you know.

HOW TO USE THIS BOOK

This book is for you if...

★ **You find it difficult to say "no"**

★ **You get quiet and shy in social situations**

★ **You worry about how you look**

★ **You avoid anything that's challenging**

★ **You feel scared of messing up**

★ **You often overthink things**

★ **You change yourself in order to fit in**

If that sounds like you – sometimes, or most of the time – this book will help. Your ability to face challenges and stand up for yourself can change, and you have the power to make those positive shifts.

Inside you'll find a host of ideas and tips on building up your self-confidence, so you can feel stronger and more comfortable being you.

This book is for and about you, so you're in charge. Take it at your own pace and if something doesn't feel like it's useful to you, it's alright to move on to the next thing. Go with what feels right for you.

PART 1:

CONFIDENCE AND YOU

WHAT IS CONFIDENCE?

Confidence
Noun

The feeling or belief that you can rely on someone or something, including yourself

Confidence is the courage to try something, even when you don't know how it's going to turn out. The more unsure you are about how it'll go, the less confident you're likely to feel. For example, your first day at a new school is likely to be pretty daunting, but by the time you've been there a few weeks, made a couple of friends and worked out where all your lessons are, you'll feel more confident each morning. It becomes less and less of a big deal.

Lots of other things can affect confidence too. It can go up or down depending on your emotions and experiences, who you're with and what's going on in your body – more on that later.

YOU ARE BEAUTIFUL;
EMBRACE IT.
YOU ARE INTELLIGENT;
EMBRACE IT.
YOU ARE POWERFUL;
EMBRACE IT.

Michaela Coel

ALL ABOUT ME

The better you know yourself, the stronger your self-confidence will be. That's because the more you learn about yourself, the more secure you feel in your choices, likes and dislikes. It gets easier to see what's important to you, and to stand up for what you care about. Here are some prompts to get you thinking about you! Write your answers in the spaces below or use an extra piece of paper if you want to write more:

My name is...

If I was stuck on a desert island, the three things I'd want with me are...

In ten years, I'll be spending my time...

One thing I find really difficult is...

Something random about me is...

My friends are...

If I knew I couldn't fail, I would...

I secretly really like...

Recently, I learned...

I wish I could...

If I could live anywhere, I'd live...

I feel good when...

WHAT HIGH SELF-CONFIDENCE FEELS LIKE

Feeling calm most of the time	Being kind to yourself	Owning up to mistakes	Being excited to learn new things
Asking for help when you need it	Taking breaks	Knowing that you're a good person	Caring for your body
Feeling OK with being single	Speaking up for yourself	Respecting others	Celebrating your achievements
Talking about your feelings	Standing up for others	Being willing to change your mind	Feeling comfortable saying "no"

WHAT LOW SELF-CONFIDENCE FEELS LIKE

Not really knowing how you feel	Needing to agree with others	Feeling angry or jealous at people's successes	Thinking you're not good enough
Comparing yourself to others	Worrying about how you look	Keeping quiet in order to fit in	Saying "yes" when you want to say "no"
Disrespecting others	Needing compliments or likes to feel OK	Not really liking your friends	Putting yourself down
Being unkind to yourself when you make a mistake	Needing other people to agree with you	Rejecting ideas before considering them properly	Thinking you need to change yourself in order to be accepted and liked

IF WE'RE ONLY GETTING OUR SELF-ESTEEM FROM THINGS OUTSIDE OURSELVES (VALIDATION FROM OTHERS, MONEY, AWARDS, ETC.) THAT'S ACTUALLY NOT SELF-ESTEEM. THAT'S OTHER-ESTEEM.

Iris McAlpin

HOW DO YOU FEEL RIGHT NOW?

Take a moment to notice how you're feeling right at this moment. You might like to close your eyes and take a deep breath as you check in with yourself.

Now consider these questions – you can write your answers here or just ponder them in your mind.

I feel...

My energy levels are...

My emotions are...

My body feels...

My mind feels...

It would feel really good to...

I'm thinking about...

THE SELF-CONFIDENCE QUIZ

Take this quiz to see how high or low your self-confidence is right now. Pick a number for each statement – if it sounds just like you, circle 5. If it's nothing like you, pick zero or 1. If you're somewhere in-between, pick the number that feels right.

I feel comfortable speaking in front of people

1 2 3 4 5

I like trying new things

1 2 3 4 5

My friends and I encourage each other

1 2 3 4 5

I feel OK about making small mistakes

1 2 3 4 5

I'm a pretty great person, just as I am

1 2 3 4 5

I speak my mind when I disagree with someone

1 2 3 4 5

21–30: you have high self-confidence! You know who you are and how to show yourself kindness. You have a good circle of friends and you all treat each other with the same respect you show yourselves. This book will help you understand and strengthen your self-confidence even more, as well as recognize the signs of low self-confidence in others.

11–20: you're doing well in terms of self-confidence, but you could do with building it up some more. You know how to give yourself a boost of positivity when you need it, which is a brilliant skill to have. Strengthening your inner sense of confidence will help you feel good about yourself, whatever happens.

0–10: your self-confidence is pretty low. You tend to put other people's feelings and needs in front of your own, and prefer to stay in your comfort zone rather than put yourself forward for something new and exciting. Your feelings matter and it's OK to take it slow – keep reading to build up your confidence and shine a little brighter.

WHAT AFFECTS YOUR SELF-CONFIDENCE?

There are loads of things that affect young people's confidence. Your mind and body change and grow a huge amount when you're a teenager, and this makes it a particularly vulnerable time for knocks to your self-confidence.

Here are just a few of the things that can affect your self-confidence:

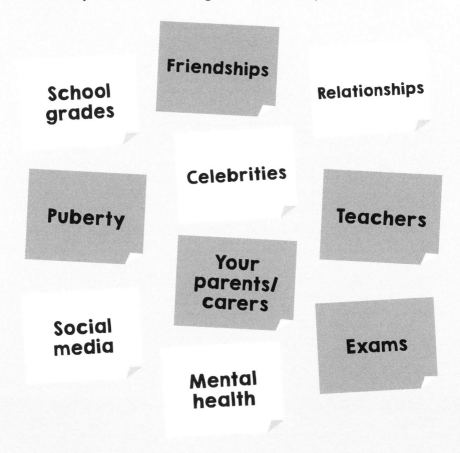

School grades

Friendships

Relationships

Celebrities

Puberty

Teachers

Your parents/carers

Social media

Exams

Mental health

Life is full of ups and downs, and your confidence will go up and down too. A healthy sense of self-confidence will mean that even if things don't go to plan or someone tries to bring you down, you'll be resilient enough to get back to feeling confident about yourself more quickly.

HOW LOW SELF-CONFIDENCE CAN AFFECT YOUR LIFE

I never felt confident enough to ask for help at school, and it meant I didn't do as well in my exams as I hoped to.

I used to love swimming, but I worry about how I look in a swimming costume so much that I don't do it any more.

Someone at school started a rumour about me, telling everyone I was a terrible person. It wasn't true but I apologized just to get them off my back.

I arranged to meet up with my boyfriend at the weekend, but he forgot about it and didn't turn up. I felt really angry and let down, but I didn't feel able to tell him how I felt. Instead I said it was no big deal.

Last year I had a best friend who would put me down all the time. He'd tell me no one else liked me and I was lucky to have him. It took me ages to ditch him because I believed what he was saying to me.

All my friends had a sleepover, but one girl was away and couldn't make it. My other friends were being really nasty about her at the sleepover. I wanted to stick up for her but I was worried they'd turn on me, so I kept quiet.

CAN YOU GO FROM LOW TO HIGH SELF-CONFIDENCE?

You definitely can! Building self-confidence can feel a bit uncomfortable at first. If it's a new idea to you, adjusting how you think and feel about yourself might seem a bit fake or forced, and acting with confidence can feel super uncomfortable if you don't yet feel that level of confidence deeply.

Everyone has a different baseline when it comes to self-confidence, so where you start is unique to you. Building stronger self-confidence means carefully considering your thoughts and actions, asking yourself questions and showing yourself a ton of patience. Slowly, the way you see yourself will shift to a more positive place.

There are ways to quickly boost your confidence (like winning a race or buying a new outfit), as well as stuff that will send your confidence levels plummeting (like failing a test or being left out by your friends), but we generally settle back to about the same confidence level once we've moved on from these temporary highs and lows.

By working on your self-confidence from the inside out, that baseline level you return to will be higher and stronger so you'll be able to feel confident in yourself, whatever happens.

HAVE CONFIDENCE THAT IF YOU HAVE DONE A LITTLE THING WELL, YOU CAN DO A BIGGER THING WELL TOO.

David Storey

PART 2:

CONFIDENCE BOOSTERS

BOOSTING YOUR SELF-CONFIDENCE

Quick and easy tricks to boost your confidence levels are really useful when you need a bit of help finding your strength and courage. These kinds of boosts help you to get out of your comfort zone, quieten negative thinking and prove to yourself how brilliant you truly are... which all lead to raising your inner self-confidence levels.

Read on to discover lots of ways to find confidence when you need it most.

WHAT MAKES YOU FEEL CONFIDENT (AND HOW CAN YOU DO MORE OF IT?)

Everyone has different things that make them feel on top of the world. Doing more of these things will help boost your confidence in the short term, and build it up in the long run. Write a list below, using the prompts to get you started:

When do you feel most confident?

Who helps you feel confident?

Where do you feel most confident?

Can you think of ways you could do more of these things?

What would it be like to do them every day?

WHAT DRAINS YOUR CONFIDENCE (AND HOW CAN YOU DO LESS OF IT?)

Some places, people and experiences just make you feel rubbish about yourself. Perhaps it's a subject at school that isn't your strongest, or a piece of clothing that you don't feel yourself in.

Can you think of two or three situations that knock your self-confidence?

Is there a way you could spend less time doing these things? If not, is there a way you could boost your confidence before, during or afterward? For example, "I can ask my best friend for a pep talk before science lessons," or "I can ask for school trousers that fit me better."

AFFIRMATIONS FOR CONFIDENCE

An affirmation is a short, positive sentence to help you challenge negative thoughts. Research has shown that when you repeat positive affirmations on a regular basis, you feel calmer and more confident. The more you repeat them, the more you believe them. Different affirmations work for different people, so give these a try and see which ones are a good fit for you.

I HAVE CONFIDENCE

I AM STRONG

I AM UNBEATABLE

I AM AMAZING

I CAN TRY MY BEST

ONE STEP AT A TIME

I DON'T HAVE TO HAVE IT ALL FIGURED OUT

I CAN DO THIS

I AM SUCCESSFUL.

I LIKE WHO I AM

I CAN USE MY VOICE

I AM TALENTED

I AM SAFE

I CAN SAY "NO"

I DESERVE RESPECT

I CAN CHANGE MY MIND

MY FEELINGS MATTER

I RESPECT MYSELF

I DESERVE THIS

I BELONG HERE

I AM THE GREATEST OF ALL TIME

Did you find one or two that make you feel that bit more confident? Remember, the key is to repeat the affirmations (out loud or in your head) as often as you can, so why not write them on sticky notes and place them where you'll see them every day? Or turn to page 131 to make an affirmation poster.

TALKING ABOUT FEELINGS

When you talk about how you're feeling with someone you trust, it really helps. But at the same time, it can be really difficult.

If you're having trouble with self-confidence, talking about your feelings probably isn't easy at all. It takes quite a lot of courage to be honest about how you're really doing, and when you're feeling down on yourself, your mind can trick you into believing that people don't care, or that your emotions aren't important.

Sadly, it's true that some people will respond unkindly when you share your thoughts and feelings with them. Not everyone is a good listener, and it's wise to choose someone you really trust and feel comfortable with – a parent, carer, teacher, friend or relative.

Talking about your feelings is really brave, and takes a lot of confidence. Finding the strength to talk openly is one of the best ways to build your self-confidence, because it shows you that other people care, helps with self-belief and demonstrates huge respect for yourself.

What's it like to talk about feelings? Some people find it pretty easy, for others it's scary, awkward or cringeworthy.

To help make it easier to talk about your feelings and mental health, try one of these conversation starters:

I feel really awkward talking about this. Can I tell you something?

Can I share a blog with you? It's really made me think.

Can I just vent for a second?

I don't need advice, just someone to talk to.

I could really use your help with something.

This might sound weird, but I've been feeling...

When you... I felt...

Is it a good time to talk? Something's been bugging me...

WHO CAN I TALK TO?

Think about the person or people in your life you trust and feel comfortable with. Write their name(s) here – what makes them a good listener?

If you don't have someone like that in your life, skip to page 138 and check out the list of resources. You're not alone and help is always available.

GIVE YOURSELF A PEP TALK

Sometimes we all need a boost of positivity from someone who believes in us. A pep talk can lift you out of a negativity hole and put you in a more confident frame of mind. The good news is, you can be the one who gives yourself a pep talk, any time you need it.

Stand in front of the mirror, and read these words to yourself. It might feel silly at first, but keep going until you get to the end.

You've got this. I believe in you. Things might not feel easy right now, but you are stronger than you think and it will all be so worth it in the end. Just keep taking it one step at a time, always moving in the right direction. Whatever happens, you'll be OK.

Why not record yourself giving a pep talk, while you're feeling pretty good? Then you can play it back to yourself whenever you need it.

MAKE A CONFIDENCE PLAYLIST

Which songs make you feel strong, confident and ready to take on the world? Perhaps some of the people on your list of confidence role models are musicians, or there's a song that makes you sit up straighter and dance around when it comes on the radio.

Use this space to plan a confidence-boosting playlist:

Listen to one or all of these songs when you want to feel like a million dollars.

NAMING FEELINGS

Did you know that naming the emotions you're feeling is really powerful? Studies have shown that when you name what you're feeling, the feeling itself becomes less intense and easier to deal with.

   So when you need a bit of extra confidence, take a moment to name what you're really feeling – out loud, in your head or by writing it down.

Sad

Anxious

Embarrassed

Frightened

Jealous

I FEEL

Alone

Confused

Angry

Stressed

Threatened

Write down what you are feeling right now:

I feel...

CONFIDENCE MEDITATION

Meditation is a really useful way to calm your mind and body, as well as boost your self-confidence. It might feel really strange at first, but the more you do it, the easier and more comfortable it gets. Meditation literally changes the structure of your brain, helping you feel calm under pressure, less easily stressed and even improving your relationships with others.

You can meditate pretty much anywhere, but a comfy chair somewhere quiet is a good place to try it out. Here's a meditation for confidence. Read it through, then go through the steps one by one.

Get comfy and set a timer for one minute, or choose a relaxing song.

Close your eyes and pay attention to your breathing. See if you can slow it down a bit.

Imagine a beam of light shining from the top of your head. The light fills you with confidence. Picture the light flowing downward until it's bathing your whole body.

Concentrate on your breathing, and the feeling of light infusing you with confidence.

When the timer runs out or the song ends, slowly open your eyes.

This is how meditation works: while your mind is focused on something like your breathing or an image, it doesn't have a chance to focus on anything else (like emotions or negative thoughts), which changes how you're feeling and what you're thinking about. So meditating is a great thing to do if you ever get stuck overthinking things, or struggling with difficult feelings.

How do you feel, right after that meditation? Circle the feelings you can relate to:

Confident

Relaxed

Bored

Silly

Uncomfortable

Sleepy

Numb

Embarrassed

Worried

Sad

Upset

However meditating made you feel is OK. It can be super weird to be alone with your thoughts all of a sudden. Just like anything else, it takes a bit of practice to get the hang of meditation. If it helped you feel that bit more confident, then it might be worth sticking with it. If it's not for you, that's OK too.

LISTEN TO YOUR THOUGHTS

What's on your mind? At any moment you might be thinking about all sorts of stuff, but is there anything bugging you or worrying you? Perhaps it's lots of random things, or something specific taking up a lot of headspace – like an upcoming test or a friend who's not texting you back. Try writing your thoughts here, on some scrap paper or in a notebook.

Often, writing your thoughts down makes you feel that little bit better. It's like you're moving your thoughts out of your head and onto the paper, giving your mind a break from thinking them. You might feel worried or embarrassed about writing your thoughts down, so remember that you don't need to show anyone at all. Once you've finished writing, you can keep what you've written, scribble it out, show someone (only if you want to) or screw it up and throw it away.

If writing down your thoughts felt good, you might find journaling helpful for building confidence. You can write whatever you like in a journal, as often as you want. It doesn't need to be anything fancy – you can get special confidence journals but a basic notebook works perfectly too.

Here's a great way to use a journal to raise your self-confidence. Draw a line down the centre of the page, like this:

On this side, write your worries and self-doubt	On this side, imagine you are a very confident person – what would you say to the thoughts in the other column?

Turn to page 48 to find your confidence role model – you can use them to inspire your answers.

Researchers have studied the reasons why writing is so good for your mental health. It helps to reduce feelings of depression, anxiety and stress because writing your thoughts down means your mind can organize and process them in a way that's difficult to do when they're stuck in your head.

BEING STRONG IS NEVER EASY.
NOT IN THIS WORLD
WE ARE LIVING IN...
STANDING UP
FOR YOURSELF
IS NOT GOING TO BE EASY,
BUT IT'S ALWAYS
EVENTUALLY
RESPECTED.

Serena Williams

WHAT IS MINDFULNESS?

Mindfulness is a way to train your brain to think more positively, calmly and confidently. It's basically about focusing all your attention on what is happening right now, in the present moment.

Mindfulness originated as a Buddhist idea, and it's been around for thousands of years. In the past 40 years it's become really popular as a tool to improve people's mental health, and lots of studies have been done on it, with amazing results.

Do you ever do dumb things when you're feeling angry, upset or excited... the kind of thing you look back on and cringe? That's because when you feel a big emotion, your limbic system (the part of the brain responsible for emotions) takes over and your cortex (the part of the brain that does the logical thinking) takes a back seat, so your actions are more influenced by how you're *feeling* and you're less able to think through their consequences or whether they're a good idea or not.

So when you practise mindfulness, it's like pressing pause so your limbic system can feel its feelings without you acting on them. The more you do this, the more comfortable you feel with your feelings, and the easier it becomes to deal with big emotions. This, in turn, makes you more confident in your choices and less likely to do something you'll later regret.

HOW TO BE MINDFUL

So, how's it done? You can do almost anything mindfully. You can walk mindfully, eat mindfully, scroll social media mindfully... You get the idea.

Here's how to take a shower mindfully:

Run the water until it's just the right temperature for you. You're going to give this shower your full attention – the shower is your whole universe for the next couple of minutes.

Get under the water and feel the sensation of it on your skin. Feel the temperature, listen to the sound of it falling, stick your tongue out and taste the warm water.

Grab your shampoo or body wash and smell it. Feel the packaging in your hand – notice its weight. Feel how it changes from liquid to bubbles in your hand. Notice how it feels in your hair and on your skin.

Pay attention to any emotions you're feeling, but just let them be.

When you're ready, turn off the water and step out of the shower. Dry yourself slowly and gently.

Now you've taken a mindful shower, you can do anything mindfully! All you need to do is slow down, pay attention to your senses and appreciate all the small details.

PICK A CONFIDENCE ROLE MODEL

When you picture a confident person, who springs to mind? They might be celebrities, fictional characters or people you know. Write their names here:

Can you pick just one to be your confidence role model?

Write your confidence role model's name in the middle, and brainstorm the words you associate with them – these might be adjectives, song lyrics, quotes or things they're well known for.

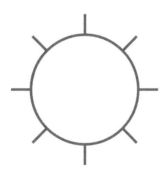

This person is your confidence role model. When you feel low in confidence, imagine they are with you, radiating courage and self-belief and guiding you to be your most confident self.

12 QUICK CONFIDENCE HACKS

1. **Listen to music** – pick a song that makes you feel strong, confident and ready to take on anything.

2. **Go outside** – a change of scenery and some fresh air on your face can snap you out of negative thinking patterns and make you feel calmer.

3. **Stretch** – stretching releases stress and tension in the body and mind, bringing you a rush of confidence.

4. **Give yourself a pep talk** – look in the mirror and remind yourself how capable you are.

5. **Bring a lucky charm** – if you believe your object is lucky, having it with you will boost your confidence and make you more likely to succeed.

6. **Doodle** – a bit of random creativity calms the mind and helps you feel more in control.

7. **Take a deep breath** – oxygen boosts confidence by bringing energy and focus to your mind and body.

8. Shake it off – imagine you're shaking the self-doubt out of your body. Jump up and down, shake your arms and legs, roll your shoulders back.

9. Hydrate – a glass of water clears the mind and makes your body feel instantly stronger and calmer.

10. Channel your confidence role model – what would they do in this situation? That's what you need to do.

11. Feel proud – think of a time you achieved something amazing, to remind yourself how brilliant you are.

12. Text a friend – share your feelings with someone you trust, and ask for words of encouragement.

YOU ARE JUST RIGHT AS YOU ARE

It might feel like you need to change into a different person in order to be confident, but that's not the case. Confidence doesn't always look like you'd think: loud, demanding and unwilling to compromise. In fact, people who behave like that often lack real confidence in themselves, because they think they need to squish down everyone else in order to get what they want.

True confidence is about knowing what you want and don't want, and calmly asserting yourself because you know you deserve it. It's saying "yes" and "no" with integrity and honesty. It's about knowing not everyone is going to agree with you, and understanding that's OK. It's about taking small steps in the right direction, and pausing before making choices so you can check you're being true to yourself.

You can be confident and quiet, confident and outspoken... however you are, you can be confident as well as being yourself.

SELF-CONFIDENCE EMERGENCY KIT

In this section we've found out loads of quick ways to boost your confidence when you need it. Now it's time to put together an emergency kit for when you need some strength in a hurry.

On this page, write the things that give you a boost. You can come back to it whenever you need to.

I can talk to...

An idea that helps me...
(e.g. thoughts aren't facts)

An activity that helps me...
(e.g. doodling)

Remember that...
(e.g. I am OK just as I am)

A song that makes me feel strong...

An affirmation that fills me with confidence...

PART 3:

OVERCOMING SELF-DOUBT

WHAT IS SELF-DOUBT?

You know when you want something, and a little voice in your head starts to explain why you can't have it, you don't deserve it or you'll fail if you try? That's self-doubt... and it's the enemy of confidence.

Luckily, that voice isn't telling the truth. It comes from anxiety and it's not the real you. With a bit of dedication, you can build up your voice of self-belief and self-confidence to drown out self-doubt.

THOUGHTS AREN'T FACTS

Often, we believe the things we think about ourselves without questioning them. They just feel like "the truth". Our thoughts are heavily influenced by our emotions, so if you're feeling good your thoughts are going to be positive, and the way you see the world and other people will likely be positive too.

We all see the world differently because we all have a unique blend of feelings and experiences influencing our view of the world, and our thoughts are just thoughts, they aren't facts. You can think anything at all – anxious thoughts, kind thoughts, angry thoughts, even impossible thoughts – but thinking something doesn't make it true. For example, you might be worried that it'll rain the day you go to the beach. Thinking these thoughts won't change the weather, but it might change your mood.

If sometimes you get stuck in self-doubting or negative thinking, it's OK – it happens to everyone. The trick is not to try and stop these thoughts, but to notice them and gently question whether they are true, fair or useful.

QUESTIONS FOR YOUR THOUGHTS

When you get caught up with negative thinking and doubting yourself, you can ask yourself these questions:

★ **Am I being fair to myself? (e.g. it's not fair to blame myself for something I have no control over)**

★ **Is it helpful to me to think this? (e.g. it's not helpful to imagine the worst possible outcome)**

★ **Is it likely to be true? (e.g. it's not likely that I'm going to be expelled for making one mistake)**

★ **Is it based on facts? (e.g. "I always fail" is not a fact)**

★ **What facts prove this thought wrong? (e.g. I have a good group of close friends)**

★ **Would I say this to my best friend? (If not, you definitely shouldn't be saying it to yourself!)**

You can think through these questions, or write your answers out in a journal or notebook.

SAY NICE THINGS TO YOURSELF - YOU'RE THE ONLY ONE LISTENING.

Gabrielle Bernstein

SPEAK AS IF...

The way you talk and think about yourself has a very powerful effect on your self-confidence. Try speaking as if you were confident, accomplished and calm... even if you're just pretending. Your mind will take in the idea and, just like affirmations, the more you speak as if you are confident, the more comfortable and natural it will start to feel.
Here are some ideas to get you started:

★ **I am about to get the top mark in this test**

★ **I will remember all my lines in the play**

★ **I find it easy to speak to new people**

★ **I feel really confident about this weekend**

★ **I'm going to stand up for myself today**

Just because "speak as if..." works, doesn't mean you should stop being honest about your true feelings and worries! Get a good balance between the two to really strengthen your self-confidence.

If there's something you've got a lot of self-doubt about at the moment, how could you "speak as if..." to help you feel more confident?

Write your thoughts here:

HOW PAST EXPERIENCES AFFECT YOUR CONFIDENCE

Your emotional brain has evolved to keep you safe. Not just from physical danger like falling out of a tree, but from emotional pain too. That's because the brain doesn't really care which kind of pain it is – it's concerned with protecting its human from being hurt in any way.

If you walked through a forest and got caught in a bear trap, your brain would make sure you felt lots of fear about forests, to try and stop it happening again. Similarly, if you had a sports coach who humiliated you in front of the whole team, your brain would make sure you really wanted to quit the team.

So what does that have to do with confidence?

Remember that mean little voice of self-doubt? Believe it or not, that's actually your brain trying to keep you safe. When you need strength and confidence to do something, that something usually involves a risk. If taking a risk has led to emotional pain in the past, your brain will try to protect you by stopping you from taking a similar risk again.

But what your emotional brain doesn't understand is that it can't actually see the future. Sure, you could live your life without taking any risks, doing the same things every day – but what a boring life it would be! Taking risks always involves the possibility of failing... but it also has the possibility of going really well, and teaching you amazing things: that can't happen if you don't try.

HOW TO RESPOND TO SELF-DOUBT

It's OK to doubt yourself – it's totally natural and everybody does it. Ignoring self-doubt sometimes works, but that can be really hard, especially if self-doubt brings up feelings of fear or anxiety in you.

The key to dealing with self-doubt so that it doesn't rule your life is to learn as much about your mind as you can. Combined with showing yourself kindness and patience, understanding your mind will help you see why you are thinking a particular thought and where it came from.

So, next time you start to doubt yourself, show those thoughts some curiosity. For example, if you're considering cancelling plans because you feel unattractive, consider where that idea has come from, and why you put that much importance on how you look to other people. Think about what you've seen on TV or social media that could have sparked off those feelings of self-doubt. The world is full of messages that can affect our self-confidence, some of which we don't even notice our brains absorbing.

Being curious about self-doubt will help you accept your thoughts without believing that they are 100 per cent true.

FIND YOUR INNER CHEERLEADER

Imagine having someone around who's always rooting for you, always has your back and is always ready with positive, encouraging words. Sounds pretty annoying, right? How about an inner voice that does that for you?

Practise being your own cheerleader by focusing on positive things about yourself that you like and are proud of.

Five things I'm good at...

_____

_____

_____

_____

_____

Five things I'm proud of...

_____

_____

_____

_____

_____

Five things I like about myself...

_____

_____

_____

_____

_____

If you're having trouble, here are some ideas to get you started:

I'm a good friend

I'm funny

I'm clever

I think deeply

I'm artistic

I'm thoughtful

I'm honest

SELF-DOUBT CIRCUIT BREAKERS

One way of stopping self-doubt in its tracks is to concentrate on your body for a few moments. Try one of these circuit-breaker exercises next time you get stuck listening to negative thoughts.

Pick an object to stare at and concentrate on keeping your eyes still for the count of ten. When you keep your eyes still, your brain can't access its full range of thoughts.

Take off your shoes and socks and place your bare feet flat on the ground. Mindfully concentrate on what you can feel with the soles of your feet. This pulls your attention as far away from your thinking mind as possible.

Stand up as tall as you can. Take a deep breath and puff out your chest. Relax your shoulders and spread your fingers wide. This confident stance will raise your confidence levels instantly.

Take five deep breaths, pressing down one nostril at a time so you breathe in and out through alternate nostrils. The deep breaths will boost your confidence and keeping track of where your fingers need to be will distract your brain.

DON'T BELIEVE EVERYTHING YOU THINK.

Allan Lokos

WRITE YOURSELF CONFIDENT

If you have a challenging day ahead of you, try some hopeful journaling. This is where you write about how you'd like the day to go. Writing in this way works the same as "speak as if..." (see page 58) because it trains your brain to expect positive outcomes rather than negative ones, making you feel more confident.

Think about what you'd like to happen in your day, what feelings you'd like to experience and what you'd like to achieve. It's important to be both hopeful but realistic – this activity isn't meant to make you feel inadequate or overburden you with expectations. Think of it more like a wish list for the day.

Give it a try here:

Today I will...

I'm going to feel...

I will achieve...

I will look after myself by...

You can try this as often as you like, in your notebook or journal.

BREAK-IT-DOWN PLANNER

Sometimes, self-doubt comes from seeing a task or goal as a huge mountain to climb, rather than a series of manageable steps you can take to reach that goal.

Say you want to save up for a new pair of trainers. To think about finding the full amount might feel quite overwhelming, but if you break it down into smaller chunks, it feels a lot more doable. You can factor in pocket money, getting paid to do chores, asking for contributions instead of birthday gifts... all of a sudden those trainers don't seem too far off after all. The same can be said for learning a new skill, writing a long essay, making a new friend or raising your self-confidence!

The secret to keeping yourself motivated through all the steps towards your goal is to celebrate each step. Don't wait until you reach the top of the mountain before feeling proud of yourself: be proud of every step you take.

Can you think of a goal you're working towards? Use this planner to break it down into steps. Make sure each step is specific (so you know when you've achieved it), realistic (so it doesn't feel like just another mountain) and give yourself a time frame to achieve it in.

For example: I have a 500-word English project due in one week

Break it down: write 100 words per day for five days, and celebrate each one by giving myself a high-five.

Monday	Tuesday	Wednesday	Thursday	Friday

How can you celebrate your achievements – big or small? Research shows that tiny celebrations help us stick to new habits because they create positive emotions. When we associate these new actions with positive emotions, we feel more motivated to do them. So, if you celebrate each small step, you're much more likely to reach your goal.

You can celebrate in whichever way feels most comfortable to you. Here are some ideas:

Give yourself a high-five

A big smile in the mirror

Think to yourself: "good job"

Put your arms in the air

Do a fist pump

Picture yourself achieving your goal

Do a victory dance

Add your own:

Step 1	Time frame
	Celebrated?

Step 2	Time frame
	Celebrated?

Step 3	Time frame
	Celebrated?

Step 4	Time frame
	Celebrated?

Step 5	Time frame
	Celebrated?

My goal:

ONE STEP
AT A TIME
IS ALL IT TAKES
TO GET YOU
THERE.

Emily Dickinson

PART 4:

HOW TO ACT WITH CONFIDENCE

THE SECRET TO CONFIDENCE

Have you ever heard the saying "fake it 'til you make it"? It means act like you know what you're doing, and eventually you *will* know what you're doing. This saying definitely applies to self-confidence, because it takes practice for acting with confidence to feel comfortable and natural, especially if you're not used to it.

LOW SELF-CONFIDENCE BEHAVIOURS

Let's take a look at all the ways low self-confidence can show up in our actions. If you recognize yourself in any of these descriptions, it doesn't mean you've done anything wrong – all of these things are really normal.

Avoidance: avoiding or choosing not to do something because you're scared of failing or making a mistake.

Zeinab loves history and knows lots about the second world war. But she skipped class the day she was meant to give a presentation, because she feels so uncomfortable with public speaking.

Hiding: keeping your achievements and unique qualities a secret from others.

Holly won a rosette for horse riding at the weekend. But she hid this fact from her friends because she was worried they'd think she was a show-off.

Perfectionism: believing everything you do should be perfect.

Jack got 90% in his mock exam. But instead of feeling relieved or proud, all he could think about was the 10% he didn't get, and how he'd have to push himself even harder for the real exam.

People-pleasing: trying to make sure everyone else is happy and calm, even if it means you're unhappy and stressed.

A teacher asked Abbie if she'd like to volunteer for the school council. It meant giving up half of her breaktimes, and Abbie didn't really want to, but she didn't feel comfortable saying "no". Abbie wishes she could quit the school council and spend more time with her friends, but she's worried she'd be letting other people down.

Aggression: treating others in a bossy, threatening or unkind way.

When someone else makes a mistake in class, Huey makes fun of them. But when Huey makes a mistake in class, he gets very angry and has to leave the room.

Attention-seeking: trying to get other people to tell you that you're a good or interesting person; trying to make people feel sorry for you; doing risky or shocking things so people take notice of you.

When Rhys first joined his school, he told his new friends that his dad was famous, so they'd think he was cool. He's had to tell loads of lies to keep up the pretence, but he's worried that his friends would dump him if they found out the truth.

Do you recognize your own actions in any of these behaviours? If you struggle with low self-confidence, it's likely that you've acted in one or two of these ways before, which is very normal and understandable. These behaviours help us feel better about ourselves for a little while by calming the fear we feel, but in the long run, they actually hurt our self-confidence.

This is because, in order for acting with confidence to start feeling comfortable and easy, we need practice. Just like anything else, your first few tries are bound to feel awkward. Your brain needs to create new, positive memories so we can say to ourselves: "Hey, I stood up for myself that time before and it went OK – I can do it again!"

Every time you fall back on one of these low self-confidence behaviours, the idea that you need to act this way in order to feel safe and comfortable gets stronger in your mind. So, when you take a chance and try acting with confidence, you risk feeling uncomfortable, but you gain the chance to change your life for the better.

Can you think of a time when low self-confidence affected your behaviour? What happened?

If you could travel back in time, would you do anything differently?

MAKE CHANGES BY PRESSING PAUSE

We've learned that the way we act has a big effect on our confidence, and perhaps recognized the ways we behave that keep our self-confidence low. So how do you begin to make changes that will grow your self-confidence?

The secret to changing your behaviour and acting with confidence is all about pressing pause. Low self-confidence behaviours happen most often when you're feeling a big, overwhelming emotion like anxiety or fear of rejection.

Pressing pause means recognizing when you're feeling this way, taking a deep breath and staying with the thoughts and feelings, rather than rushing to make them go away. You are safe to feel uncomfortable feelings, and they are often a sign that you're acting with courage.

How to press pause:

★ **Stop what you're doing (if it's safe to do so)**

★ **Put your hand on your heart and take a deep breath in and out**

★ **Say to yourself (out loud, in your head or written down): "I'm feeling........." e.g. scared, angry, guilty**

★ **Notice where in your body you're feeling the emotion**

★ **Notice your thoughts and remember that thoughts are not facts**

★ **If you feel the urge to do one of the low self-confidence behaviours, you can say, think or write: "I really want to............ but I won't"**

★ **Take three more deep breaths in and out**

How do you feel after pressing pause? Those feelings of discomfort and the urge to act might not have gone away completely, but hopefully they will feel more manageable.

Here's an example of how pressing pause helps you act with confidence.

Louis and Grace are in the same tutor group. One day at break, Louis accidentally bumps into Grace, hurting her shoulder. Usually, Louis would become aggressive and blame Grace for what happened, but instead he presses pause.

He takes a deep breath and thinks to himself, "I'm feeling embarrassed for making a mistake, and scared that I'll be blamed and punished. My face feels hot and I'm breathing really quickly. I really want to shout at Grace and make it seem like it's her fault." He takes three more deep breaths and says: "I'm really sorry Grace. Are you OK?"

Grace says, "Thanks for apologizing – I know it was an accident but you hurt my shoulder."

Louis offers to carry Grace's bag to their next lesson.

After that, Louis realizes that it's OK to take responsibility when you make a mistake, even when it's scary. He begins to treat others with more respect, and isn't so hard on himself when he messes up, either.

BEING ASSERTIVE

Assertive
Adjective

Acting in a way that's calm, confident and respectful to both yourself and others.

Choosing to act with confidence and resist the temptation to let low self-confidence affect how you behave takes a lot of courage, as well as a lot of trial and error. Assertiveness is a word we use to describe the sweet spot between respecting yourself and respecting other people – when you're being assertive, you're acting with confidence.

When you're assertive, you speak up for yourself without silencing others. You say "yes" and "no" and really mean it. You own up to mistakes and you speak up when someone has hurt you.

Tips for being assertive

Use "I" statements like "I feel..." and "I prefer..." rather than "you" statements.

Ask for time to think if you're not sure how to respond.

Ask for help when you need it.

Practise giving your opinion on small things, like songs or movies.

Remind yourself that your opinions matter just as much as anyone else's.

Notice if you interrupt, and apologize.

Disagree with ideas and offer your own opinion, rather than putting down the person who's voicing them.

Take responsibility for your actions.

Be clear about what you want.

Remember that you deserve respect, even when you make a mistake.

Practise saying "no" as well as phrases like "that's not going to work for me".

THE ONLY THING THAT MATTERS IN LIFE IS YOUR OWN OPINION OF YOURSELF.

Osho

SAYING "NO"

"No" is one of the hardest but most important words in your vocabulary. It takes a lot of confidence to say "no", especially if you feel pressure from others to say "yes".

You are allowed to say "no" to anything that doesn't feel right to you, even if it upsets, annoys or inconveniences someone else. The expert on how you feel, what you like and what you don't like is you. Similarly, other people are allowed to say "no" to you, and you are allowed to feel upset about it too.

Sometimes, people might try to change your "no" into a "yes". If you're ever unsure about whether to say "yes" or "no" to something, you can use this flowchart to help you decide.

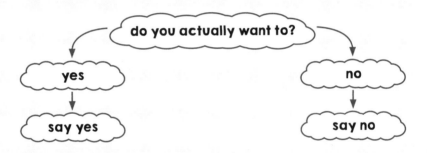

It really is that simple!

When it comes to your body, you have the right to say "no" to anyone, for any reason or no reason at all.

For things like school work and house rules, compromise is important. If something doesn't sit right with you and you want to say "no" to it, you can! Stand up for yourself by asking questions, explaining why you're uncomfortable or why it's not working for you. You deserve to have your views heard and respected.

Get more comfortable with the word "no" by
spending some time colouring in this page.

GET CHATTING

When you're feeling low on self-confidence, communicating with others can be really hard. Even making small talk can feel intimidating, especially if it's with someone you don't know very well.

It helps to have a few conversation ideas up your sleeve. Knowing you have these ready in an emergency will make you feel more confident talking to new people and hanging out with friends. People love random questions that make them think, and they can spark off funny and interesting conversations. Practise these on your family to build your conversation skills.

If you could live anywhere, where would you choose?

What would you do if you found £1 million in your pocket?

Would you rather have webbed fingers or hoofed feet?

If you could only have one meal for the rest of your life, what would it be?

If you had a theme tune, what would it be?

Who is your oldest friend, and
how did you meet them?

If you were to start a business,
what would it be?

Do you think aliens exist?

Can you think of more?

CONFIDENCE ACTION PLAN

Now you've learned all about how assertiveness will help you act with confidence, and how acting with confidence leads to feeling confident, it's time to think about how you can put it into action. Think about a situation where you find yourself acting with low self-confidence – perhaps one you wrote about on page 76?

How could you use what you've learned to act with assertiveness and confidence? Write your ideas here – you could even write a script for yourself:

Example of a script for confidence:

If Evie asks me to hang out at breaktime, I will say, "No, thank you."

If she tries to guilt me into hanging out, I will say, "I'm having lunch with Summer today."

If she won't respect that, I can walk away.

YOU NEVER KNOW
IF YOU CAN ACTUALLY
DO SOMETHING
AGAINST ALL ODDS
UNTIL YOU ACTUALLY
DO IT.

Abby Wambach

PART 5:

TAKING GOOD CARE OF YOURSELF

SELF-CARE AND SELF-CONFIDENCE

Taking good care of yourself is a big part of becoming more self-confident. Think about it – how much more confident do you feel when you're hydrated, well rested and relaxed?

The better care you take of your body and mind, the more you'll be able to calmly handle whatever life throws at you. What's more, self-care is about showing yourself the respect you deserve. Read on to find out how to look after yourself and grow your confidence at the same time.

WHAT'S THE DIFFERENCE BETWEEN MENTAL AND PHYSICAL HEALTH?

Physical health is about how well our bodies are – there are usually symptoms to alert us to physical health problems and treatments or medicine doctors can offer to help with them. Mental health is a little more complicated. It's about our thoughts and emotions, and how they affect our lives. Doctors know a lot less about mental health because it's more difficult to study, and shows up differently in everyone.

Illness or disability can affect your mental health – think about how rubbish you feel when you've got a cold – and your mental health can have an impact on your physical health too. The nervous system links the brain to every part of the body, and it's where we feel emotions. So when you do something that makes your body feel good – like yoga or drinking a glass of water – that good feeling includes your mind too.

Self-care is about taking care of both your physical and mental health, because they are so closely linked. When you take care of one, you take care of the other, even without trying!

STAY HYDRATED

Did you know, the way your body feels when you're experiencing anxiety is very similar to the way it feels when you haven't had enough water? A dry mouth, racing heart and feeling too hot might mean you're in need of a confidence boost... or a glass of water. The best part is, having a drink of water will help, whatever it is that's causing you to feel flustered.

Studies have shown that drinking water increases focus, lowers your heart rate and boosts your energy – all contributing to a more confident you. It's a good idea to keep a bottle of water in your bag all the time, so you can stay hydrated all day. Experts recommend drinking about 2 litres (eight tall glasses) of water per day.

Don't worry if water's not your thing – you can make it more appetizing by infusing it. Try this infused water recipe:

You will need:
Large jug (that fits in your fridge)
A handful of fresh or frozen fruit, herbs or vegetables
Still or sparkling water

Mix and match your favourites from this list:

Cucumber
Mint leaves
Strawberries
Mango
Orange
Lemon
Grapefruit

Method:

★ Chop the fruit, herbs and/or vegetables into thumb-sized pieces and place them in the jug.

★ Pour water into the jug.

★ Leave overnight in the fridge to infuse.

★ Strain through a sieve into a glass or bottle, and enjoy!

EATING WELL

There's a lot of information out there about how to eat healthily (check out page 139 for resources), and there's also a lot of advertising telling you to eat stuff that's not so healthy. This book isn't here to tell you what to eat. It's here to tell you that you can trust your body to tell you when it's hungry, when it's full and what it needs.

If you were throwing a dinner party for your closest friends, what would be on the menu?

MENU

If you find yourself eating less or more than feels right for you, or that food is affecting your mental health, support is available. You can reach out for help from a trusted adult, or check out page 138 for a list of places you can turn to.

MAKE YOUR OWN CALMING PUTTY

Having something for your hands to play with is a great stress and anxiety reliever. If you're feeling nervous, play with this DIY putty to help you get back in control. Adding citrusy essential oils will boost its confidence-enhancing powers, because your sense of smell is linked to the area of your brain that processes emotions.

You will need:

Palm-sized piece of sticky tack

Two squirts of liquid hand soap

Grapefruit, lemon or orange essential oil (optional)

Method:

★ **Knead the sticky tack with your fingers until it's soft and warm.**

★ **Add the liquid hand soap and continue to knead it into the sticky tack.**

★ **When it feels stretchy and all the soap is combined, add three or four drops of essential oil.**

Keep your putty in an airtight container and it will stay stretchy for two to three days. When it loses its stretch, add a little more liquid soap to refresh. Play with the putty any time you want to feel relaxed and confident.

YOU ARE POWERFUL AND YOUR VOICE MATTERS.

Kamala Harris

UNPLUG YOURSELF

Technology is brilliant: we couldn't be without it. But it's important to spend time away from screens each day, in order to connect with yourself, as well as giving your eyes and mind a break.

How do you like to unwind away from screens? Here are some ideas – add your own!

Drawing

Doodling

Reading a book

Chatting to friends and family

Running

Walking

Gardening

Team sports

Caring for animals

Caring for houseplants

Writing

Playing cards or board games

Playing with pets

Unplugging at a regular time each day is great for your confidence. The online world can sap confidence because it shows a distorted version of reality. When you step away from screens, it's easier to appreciate the smaller things and see what's really important.

Jot down your weekly routine here – can you plan screen-free time each day?

Monday	Tuesday	Wednesday	Thursday

Friday	Saturday	Sunday

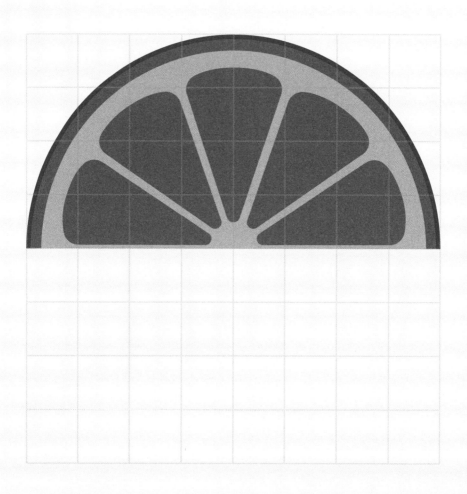

EXERCISE YOUR MIND

Challenging yourself regularly will help build your confidence, let go of perfectionism and prepare you for unexpected challenges. Try this fun drawing game to give your brain a workout.

Using your non-dominant hand (if you're right-handed, your non-dominant hand is your left hand, and if you're left-handed, it's your right), draw the other half of this orange.

It's harder than you think! This exercise is good for building confidence because it lets you practise being imperfect at something low risk. The more your brain gets comfortable with doing things imperfectly, the more self-confident you'll feel when it's time to try something new.

EXERCISE YOUR BODY

Physical exercise produces endorphins – brain chemicals that reduce pain and increase happiness. You get a rush of these chemicals when you laugh or get excited too. So even a small amount of exercise will give you a boost of confidence and energy.

When thinking about exercise, it's important to choose something that you enjoy. When you enjoy something, you're more likely to do it regularly. It sounds obvious, but a lot of people talk about exercise like it's a chore or even something that hurts. When you're getting the most out of exercise, it will feel fun, simple and pleasurable.

**What types of exercise do you do?
Write them here.**

Are there any types of exercise that you'd like to try, but feel unsure about? Write them here.

How about these?

Yoga   Swimming   Martial arts

Trampolining   Rock climbing   Cycling

Find out about after-school clubs and ask your friends about clubs you can go to. They're designed to be friendly, welcoming and you won't need any experience. Bring a friend along to give you extra confidence!

YOGA STRETCHES

Yoga is one of the best forms of exercise for mental health and confidence. Because it's slow, gentle and non-competitive, it calms the mind and body while allowing you to focus on yourself.

Starting your day with a simple yoga stretch will help you set a positive tone for the day. If you practise regularly with some simple poses like the ones here, you'll slowly feel your body become stronger and more flexible. Try this stretch first thing in the morning to release tension and fill yourself with confidence.

Stand with your feet hip-width apart. Stand tall and strong, with your palms facing forward. Breathe in through your nose, and out through your mouth.

Lace your fingers together behind your back and pull them down away from your head. Push your chest up and take a deep breath in through your nose and out through your mouth.

BREATHE IN CONFIDENCE, BREATHE OUT SELF-DOUBT

KEEPING FRESH AND CLEAN

You don't need fancy or expensive products to make sure your hair and skin are well cared for. Many beauty companies want you to believe that their product will give you clear skin and shiny hair, but they do this in order to make money. The truth is your skin and hair type are down to your genetics and aren't really a good indicator of how often you shower or what face cream you use. In fact, some ingredients you'll find in skin and haircare products – like alcohol, for example – actually strip the natural oils from your skin and hair, meaning your body produces more of them, giving you greasy hair and skin.

Keeping your routine simple and stress-free means you're sorted when it comes to hygiene. If you're prone to spots, try this simple remedy to help them heal up more quickly.

COCONUT HEALING CREAM

You will need:

2 tbsp organic coconut oil

1 tsp bicarbonate of soda

Method:

★ **Mix the two ingredients together to form a gritty paste.**

★ **Apply a small amount to a spot using the tip of your finger.**

★ **Keep in an airtight container and it will stay fresh for up to a month.**

Keep the cream away from your eyes and do not use on sensitive or broken skin.

NAVIGATING PUBERTY

During your teenage years, your body changes a lot and it can be the source of a lot of self-doubt and anxiety. It might even feel like everyone else is finding it easy while you're confused or struggling. It's important to remember that just because your body is changing, it doesn't mean that you can't have feelings, questions or worries about it. You can always talk to a trusted adult if there's anything you're unsure of or worried by – whether it's about your own body, or something someone else has said or done.

Here are some tips on keeping self-confidence high while going through puberty:

★ **Your body is yours alone, and you are the expert on how you feel. If anyone touches, comments or stares at your body in a way that makes you feel uncomfortable or unsafe at any time, it's not your fault. You can report this to the police or a trusted adult.**

★ **Be patient with your body – everyone grows at a different rate and there's no set timeline for puberty. Remember that it's not a race or a competition.**

★ **Masturbation is normal, healthy and a brilliant way to build confidence in your body. Getting to know what does and doesn't feel good for you is an important part of growing up.**

★ **Be mindful of stereotypes. Some people will make assumptions about your personality, intelligence, likes or dislikes based on how your body looks – they're wrong to do this. You are allowed to be yourself no matter what your body looks like.**

★ **Stay in touch with your body by keeping active. This helps to build self-confidence as it allows you to focus on what your body can do, rather than how it looks.**

★ **Talk and listen to older siblings, parents, carers and relatives – all of them have been through puberty and will have words of comfort, wisdom and support for you.**

A GOOD NIGHT'S SLEEP

Getting enough sleep makes such a difference to your confidence levels the next day. Think about how much more in control and positive you feel when you've had eight or more hours' sleep. A good night's sleep comes from a good night-time routine, because your body and mind need time to wind down before you can fall asleep.

WHAT MAKES FOR A GOOD NIGHT-TIME ROUTINE?

Getting ready for bed is all about sending signals to your body and mind that it's time for resting and relaxing. Here's a guide to making a good night-time routine:

★ **Avoid bright lights, including screens, for an hour before bedtime**

★ **Use soothing scents like lavender and chamomile pillow spray or herbal tea**

★ **Change into comfy clothes or pyjamas**

★ **Pick calming activities like bathing, reading, journaling and drawing**

What's your night-time routine?

Do you feel like it could be more relaxing in any way? What changes could you make? For example, turning off your phone or tablet earlier, or having an evening bath.

LOVE THE SKIN YOU'RE IN

Everyone's skin is different, and teenage skin can be extra sensitive. If your skin is prone to spots or dryness, and if you have scarring or a skin condition, it can be tough to feel confident when you're having a flare-up.

A lot of advertising and beauty advice is geared towards covering up or getting rid of any skin "imperfections", but it's important to remember that your skin is OK exactly as it is. If you want to, you can look for ways to reduce flare-ups at the same time as accepting your skin for how it is on any given day: the two don't cancel each other out.

The truth about skin is that what it looks like is largely out of your control. Many people falsely believe that any skin "issues" are down to cleanliness or not using the correct product, but in fact excessive washing damages skin and makes any dryness, oiliness or spots worse.

If you're struggling with any aspect of your skin – pain, discomfort or mental health concerns – it's a good idea to see your GP. You can also turn to page 138 for resources and places to turn for support.

SKIN PORTRAIT

Pick a patch of your skin – it could be on your hand, your tummy, your face... anywhere! Study it closely and draw or paint it here:

Treating your body with respect and interest will help build body-confidence.

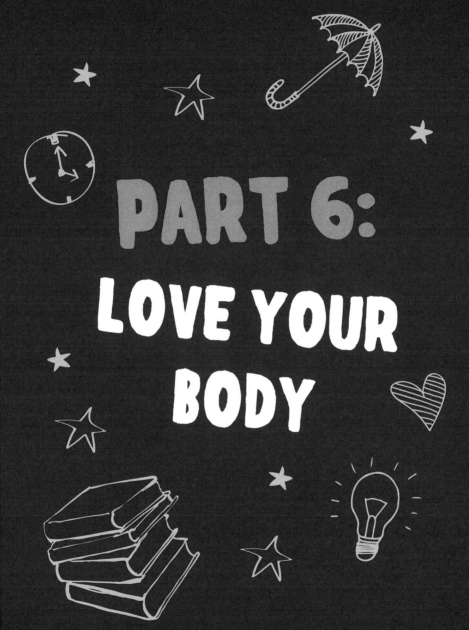

PART 6:
LOVE YOUR BODY

HOW TO BUILD BODY CONFIDENCE

Your confidence is closely linked to how you feel about your body. If you're worried about how you look, this can take your focus away from how capable you are, and drain your confidence in the process.

If you think you need to have a "perfect" body before you can feel confident, you've got it upside-down. Being comfortable in your body – however it looks – and not comparing yourself to others are at the heart of self-confidence. Your body is OK exactly as it is, and so is everyone else's.

THE MYTH OF THE PERFECT BODY

Looking at the internet, it might seem like there's one way your body is supposed to look, and if your body is different to that in any way, that's a negative thing that needs to be changed. The message that your body needs to be a certain way is everywhere. Big companies in the beauty, fashion and plastic surgery industries make lots of money from people (especially women and girls, but increasingly boys and men too) feeling insecure in their bodies, so they invest in advertising that subtly influences how we feel about ourselves, to make us buy more of their products. Sneaky, right?

The truth is, there is no such thing as a perfect body, and *your* body is fine as it is. The idea that you need to wear make-up, buy uncomfortable clothes, shave your body hair or change your body shape in order to be acceptable or attractive is a load of nonsense made up to make money for big companies. A lot of the time, young people themselves put pressure on each other to conform, because so many of us believe in the myth of the perfect body.

It's not easy, but noticing when you're believing there's something wrong with your body is the first step to feeling truly body confident. It's totally OK if wearing make-up or certain clothes gives you a boost and helps you find strength and bravery – you are free to use these confidence tools in any way you like. What's important is that you remember that you are just right, exactly as you are.

AFFIRMATIONS FOR BODY CONFIDENCE

Try these body-confident affirmations to remind yourself how precious your body is. Why not write your favourites on sticky notes and stick them on your mirror?

I belong

I am good

My body is mine

I am more than my appearance

I accept myself

I am loved as I am

My body is strong

I feel good

I am confident

I do not exist for other people to look at

I AM
MINE.
BEFORE
I AM EVER
ANYONE
ELSE'S.

Nayyirah Waheed

KEEP A GRATITUDE JOURNAL

Taking time each day to think about the good things in your life that you feel thankful for is a really powerful way to build confidence. The more positively you view yourself and your life, the better and stronger you'll feel about yourself.

Try writing in this gratitude journal every day for a week:

MONDAY

I'm grateful to my body for...

A person I'm grateful for...

I'm grateful that...

TUESDAY

I'm grateful to my body for...

A person I'm grateful for...

I'm grateful that...

WEDNESDAY

I'm grateful to my body for...

A person I'm grateful for...

I'm grateful that...

THURSDAY

I'm grateful to my body for...

A person I'm grateful for...

I'm grateful that...

FRIDAY

I'm grateful to my body for...

A person I'm grateful for...

I'm grateful that...

SATURDAY

I'm grateful to my body for...

A person I'm grateful for...

I'm grateful that...

SUNDAY

I'm grateful to my body for...

A person I'm grateful for...

I'm grateful that...

DRESSING FOR CONFIDENCE

The type of clothes that make you feel confident are different for everybody. Perhaps you feel amazing when you dress smartly, or at your best in comfy jeans. The key is to feel like the best version of yourself – if you don't feel yourself, there's no way you'll feel self-confident.

What outfit makes you feel strong and confident? Draw it here. It might be an outfit you have already, or one you'd love to wear one day.

Pick clothes that make you feel comfortable and confident, whatever you have planned.

SELF-CARE TOOLKIT

What do you do to take care of your body and mind? What feels good and contributes to your well-being is very personal, so take some time to think about what works for you.

Write about the things you do every day and every week, plus the self-care you can show yourself when you need extra care.

Every day I can...
[examples: take a shower, walk, say an affirmation]

Every week I can...
[examples: do some yoga, chat with my best friend]

When I need a boost of confidence, I can...
[examples: give myself a pep talk, wear my confident outfit]

When I want to show myself extra care, I will...
[examples: go for a swim, watch my favourite movie]

I TRY NOT TO
LET THE MEDIA
TRICK ME INTO
FEELING LIKE THERE'S
SOMETHING WRONG WITH
HOW I LOOK –
AS LONG I'M HEALTHY
AND FEEL GOOD
I DON'T SEE
WHAT THE PROBLEM IS.

Ming Bridges

PART 7:

BE TRUE TO YOURSELF

YOU ARE YOUR OWN BEST FRIEND

Being true to yourself is about staying tuned in to your feelings and standing up for yourself. What's popular isn't always what's right for you, and it can be really difficult to stay true to yourself sometimes, especially if you feel pressured by those around you to fit in.

In this chapter we'll look at ways to identify what's important to you, and tools for staying true to yourself, no matter what.

WHAT ARE BOUNDARIES?

Boundaries are rules you set about how other people can treat you. They're different for everyone, and they're a way of confidently communicating what's OK and not OK for you personally. Boundaries are useful for building respectful friendships and relationships.

Here are some examples of boundaries:

> *I don't eat meat.*

> *If someone swears at me, I will end the conversation straight away.*

> *I can stay until 4 p.m.*

> *You're making me feel uncomfortable. Can you please stop that?*

You get to decide what you will and won't do with your body, what kind of conversations you're comfortable having and how long you stay in any particular situation. You will have different boundaries with different people, and your boundaries are totally based on what you feel comfortable with – you don't have to be able to explain why.

Many of us aren't used to firm boundaries, and they can feel quite scary – whether you're the one setting the boundary or someone is communicating their boundary with you. However, as American therapist Elizabeth Earnshaw puts it, "When people set boundaries with you, it's their attempt to continue the relationship with you. It's not an attempt to hurt you."

TIPS FOR SETTING BOUNDARIES

Think back to what you learned about assertiveness on page 79 – setting boundaries is a great time to practise assertiveness. If you're not used to it, setting boundaries can feel really intimidating and fill you with self-doubt; because of this, it's a brilliant exercise in feeling the fear and doing it anyway. The more you set boundaries, the more confident you will feel next time you do it.

Here are some tips to help you navigate boundaries with confidence:

Say exactly what you mean and be specific – remember, people can't read your mind.

If someone gets angry and tries to make you change your mind about a boundary, that's a sign you were right to set it – you don't need to back down.

If a friend keeps disrespecting your boundaries, consider whether you want to keep them as a friend.

If someone accuses you of being too sensitive or too serious because of your boundaries, this is a sign they feel embarrassed about their behaviour. You don't need to take their words to heart.

If someone sets a boundary with you and it hurts, it's OK to feel that way. You can respect their boundary as well as taking care of your own feelings.

It's OK to rethink a boundary if you want to give someone a second chance — you're in charge.

WHAT ARE YOUR VALUES?

Personal values are the characteristics that we aspire to have, the way we want to act and that we value in ourselves and look for in other people. When you stay true to your values, you can act with confidence even if it feels uncomfortable or you're unsure how other people will respond.

Knowing who you are and what's important to you will give you strength and a solid foundation to build a more confident you. Take some time to work out what your values are by having a go at this exercise.

Below are lots of examples of personal values. Can you choose the ten that you think are the most important to you?

If there's a characteristic you value that isn't included here, feel free to add it yourself.

Achievement   Adventure   Courage

Creativity   Dependability   Determination

Friendship   Health   Honesty

Independence   Integrity   Intelligence

Justice   Kindness   Learning   Love

Peace   Security   Simplicity

Spontaneity   Success   Understanding

Wealth   Ambition   Family   Fun

Hard work   Charity   Education

Empathy   Loyalty   Respect   Truth

Teamwork   Popularity   Open-mindedness

Faith   Generosity

When you've chosen them, write your top ten values here:

_____

_____

_____

_____

_____

_____

_____

_____

_____

_____

Now here's the real challenge: can you narrow your list down to just your five most important values?

_____

_____

_____

_____

_____

What have you discovered about your values by doing this exercise? Your values can change as you grow, and that's OK – the things you value right now are important. If you're ever in a difficult situation and you're not sure what to do, thinking about how you could act in line with your values will help you work it out.

FINDING A MIDDLE GROUND

Compromise
noun

A settlement of a dispute that is reached by each side making concessions

When there's a disagreement or argument, sometimes it's a case of right and wrong. But more often, both people have a valid opinion; when this happens, compromise is a great skill to have. When we compromise, we recognize that neither person is completely right or completely wrong, and find a solution both can agree on.

Let's say you have plans to meet up with a friend on Saturday, but you want to do different things. Do you...

a. Insist on your idea

b. Do your own thing, even if it means doing it alone

c. Go along with their idea

d. Find something else that you'd both enjoy doing

If you answered D, that's compromise. In this case, you can stand up for yourself while still showing understanding to your friend – a sign of true confidence.

There are other times when compromise isn't the right way to go. If you find yourself agreeing to things you don't believe or that make you feel unsafe, it's OK to stand your ground. For example, if someone wants to take you out on a date and you don't like them, you don't need to find a different type of date, or be their friend: you can simply say "no thank you". Compromise should feel comfortable for everyone involved.

ALL ABOUT COMPARISON

We all compare ourselves to others – it's part of being human. It's also a real drain on confidence! Measuring your appearance, strengths or achievements against other people's will ultimately leave you feeling rubbish about yourself. Even if you think you're doing better than someone else, basing your self-confidence on where other people are in comparison with you will mean your confidence can plummet as soon as you see someone else succeeding.

So how can you stop comparing? The key is to get comfortable with yourself, build your confidence up and recognize the fact that you never know anyone else's full story. When you feel strong and self-confident, seeing other people doing well won't bother you so much – you'll realize that there's room for everybody. It's also very possible that other people are comparing themselves with you – after all, we only ever see other people's highlight reel. Someone might see your gaming skills and think they come naturally... they don't know about all the practice and *game overs* that got you there.

If you notice yourself comparing, take a moment to find your inner strength and self-confidence. Remind yourself that you and everyone else is unique and complicated, and that you don't know their full story.

Try this: write down three things that make you, you

GOOD FRIEND, BAD FRIEND

Friendships have a big effect on confidence. If you spend most of your time around people who support you and love you for who you are, your confidence is naturally boosted.

Not everyone is a good fit for you, and that's OK. There are a few things you can look out for when you're getting to know someone (or even if you've known them a long time), to see if they're a positive person to have around. These characteristics count for friends, romantic relationships, teammates... anyone you spend time with.

a good friend...	a bad friend...
Feels comfortable to be around	Puts you down for being yourself
Is happy for you to choose your other friends	Controls who you see
Replies to your messages	Ignores or ghosts you
Is considerate of your feelings	Treats you like your feelings don't matter
Is interested in your thoughts, feelings and experiences	Is not interested in what you have to say
Makes you feel safe	Makes you feel anxious or unsafe
Laughs with you	Laughs at you
Listens when you tell them they've upset you	Refuses to acknowledge that they've upset you
Wants to hang out with you	Drops you for other plans

Sometimes, people start out as a good friend, then switch to treating you badly later on. If you're in a friendship or relationship where you feel unhappy, unsafe or like you can't leave, it's not your fault. You deserve to feel happy and comfortable in all of your friendships and relationships.

There are many people you can talk to if you're unsure about someone in your life – a trusted friend, teacher or family member is a good place to start. You can also turn to page 138 for more resources and information.

MY FRIENDS

Who are your closest friends? Draw or stick pictures of them here, then add their name and one thing that makes them a great friend underneath.

CONFIDENCE FOR LIFE

Having good friends now will help form the blueprint for friendships and relationships later on. If you're reading this book and feeling worried about how others might respond to you if you start acting with greater self-confidence, you're not alone.

Some people might react badly when you grow in confidence and assertiveness. The difficult truth is, this is a really quick way to tell who respects you and who doesn't. If you lose a friend because you stood up for yourself, that person likely wasn't a very good friend to have around.

On the flip side, good friends will support you showing your inner strength and your true self. The more time you spend around supportive, respectful people, the more you'll expect it when you meet someone new.

Imagine yourself in ten years: you're strong, confident and flourishing.

What kind of friends will you have?

Where will you live?

Will you be studying, have a job or something else?

MAKE AN AFFIRMATION POSTER

Have you found an affirmation that boosts your self-confidence? There are lots to choose from on pages 32–33 and page 112, or you can come up with your own.

Use this space to cut out and make a poster of your favourite affirmation. You could use cool lettering, bright colours and illustrations to make it really eye-catching.

Why not stick your poster up by your bed so you'll see it when you wake up each morning?

SPEAK THE TRUTH, EVEN IF YOUR VOICE SHAKES.

Maggie Kuhn

PART 8:

LOOKING FORWARD

A STRONG FUTURE

As you grow, your self-confidence will naturally go up and down. Some days you'll feel unstoppable – enjoy those days; you deserve them. Other days will be harder. You'll doubt yourself, be disappointed, or other people will try to bring you down. This happens to everybody and it's part of living a full life.

In this final section you'll find ideas and resources to take forward with you. Strong, healthy self-confidence is a lifelong project, and getting into good habits while you're a teen is the greatest gift you can give your future self.

YOU'RE NOT ALONE

Many young people struggle with low self-confidence. Here are some of their stories:

On holiday in Turkey there was this banana boat that took you round the bay. Every day my brothers went on the banana boat but I stayed behind with my parents. It looked really fun but I was so worried about falling off. They'd invite me but were fine about it when I said no. I watched them all have a great time and never saw anyone get hurt. On the last day I plucked up the courage to go with my brothers. I was nervous at first, but it was so much fun.

Aisling, 11

I had a job at a café in the kitchen - clearing tables and operating the dishwasher, that kind of thing. It was OK money but they kept asking me to stay later without paying for my time, and I'd do it because I thought I was lucky to have a job at all. I mentioned it to my mum, and she reminded me my time was precious and it was the café that was lucky to have me, not the other way around. I told my boss I wouldn't be doing any more unpaid work and he said I had to if I wanted to keep my job... so I quit. I now have a much better job where I'm treated with respect.

Lucas, 16

I competed in a horse-riding competition last year, but I fell off my horse during one of the jumps. I wasn't badly hurt but it was so embarrassing - everyone saw and the photographer got a photo right as I hit the ground. All my confidence just disappeared, but I didn't give up. I had some one-to-one lessons, then started riding with a group to get my confidence back. Now I feel ready for the next competition.

Florence, 14

STRONGER THAN YOU KNOW RULES TO LIVE BY

You are OK exactly as you are

Messing up and trying again is how we learn

Spend your time with respectful people

Take good care of your body and mind

Stand up for yourself, even when it's hard

Feel the fear and do it anyway

Trust your judgement

You are loved

ASKING FOR HELP

If you're struggling with low self-confidence, or any other aspect of your mental health, there are lots of organizations out there you can turn to for help and advice. If you feel like your confidence is starting to have a negative effect on your life, it's a good idea to talk to a trusted adult and make an appointment with your doctor.

Be Real Campaign
berealcampaign.co.uk
Campaign to change attitudes towards body image, encouraging people to put health above appearance and feel body confident.

BEAT
0808 801 0711
www.beateatingdisorders.org.uk
Helpline, webchat and online support groups for people with eating disorders, such as anorexia and bulimia.

British Nutrition Foundation
nutrition.org.uk
Information and advice on healthy, sustainable eating habits.

Campaign Against Living Miserably (CALM)
0800 58 58 58
thecalmzone.net
Provides listening services, information and support for anyone who needs to talk, including a web chat.

Childline
0800 1111
childline.org.uk
Support for young people in the UK, including a free 24-hour helpline.

FRANK
0300 123 6600
talktofrank.com
Confidential advice and information about drugs, their effects and the law.

The Jed Foundation
1 800 273 8255
jedfoundation.org
Information and advice for US teens to promote emotional and mental health.

National Alliance on Mental Illness (NAMI)
1 800 950 6264
nami.org
Information and advice on managing mental health for US teens.

My Plate
myplate.gov
Information and resources for healthy eating.

On My Mind
annafreud.org/on-my-mind
Information for young people to make informed choices about their mental health and well-being.

Refuge
0808 2000 247
refuge.org.uk
Advice and support for domestic abuse.

This Girl Can
thisgirlcan.co.uk
Website and app to celebrate and encourage women and girls' participating in sport and exercise.

Young Minds
youngminds.org.uk
Information about every aspect of mental well-being for young people.

FURTHER READING

Check out these books for teens about confidence, mental health and inner strength:

Staying Fat for Sarah Byrnes
Chris Crutcher

Be True to Yourself
Amanda Ford

The Confidence Code for Girls
Claire Shipman and Katty Kay

Just As You Are
Michelle and Kelly Skeen

The Think Confident, Be Confident Workbook for Teens
Leslie Sokol and Marci Fox

Wolfpack
Abby Wambach

The Self-Care Kit for Stressed-Out Teens
Frankie Young

CONCLUSION

You are good enough, even when you don't feel like it. Building inner strength and self-confidence can be hugely challenging, and it's OK to take your time, make mistakes and keep learning. Trusting yourself enough to step forward, even if you don't know how things will turn out, is the best and truest way to a strong, confident you.

It takes a whole heap of courage to stand up for yourself and be the self-assured young person you are inside. Taking small steps every day toward confidence will show you just how capable you really are.

Remember: you are stronger than you know!

Am I GOOD ENOUGH? YES I AM.

Michelle Obama

NO MORE WORRIES!

Paperback

£10.99

978-1-78783-935-9

Do you worry a lot?

Your teens are full of new challenges – peer pressure, exams, wondering what the future holds and everything in between. It's normal to feel anxious sometimes, but when it starts to affect your health and happiness it's time to show worry the door and get your life back on track. *No More Worries!* contains top tips and activities to help you alleviate the symptoms of anxiety and feel better equipped to cope when it strikes, while remaining positively you.

YOU'VE GOT THIS!

Paperback

£10.99

978-1-78685-801-6

Do you often feel you're not good enough?

Your teens are full of new challenges – exams, peer pressure, planning your future and anything and everything in between. This can turn every day into a minefield of emotions and lead to one big headache. How you feel about yourself in all this chaos can make life even tougher. When you think you don't measure up, it can be hard to pick yourself up again, but when you feel good about yourself, you can approach every situation with confidence and say "I've got this!" This book contains top tips and activities to help your self-esteem flourish and make you proud to be awesomely you.

Have you enjoyed this book?
If so, why not write a review on your favourite website?

If you're interested in finding out more about our books,
find us on Facebook at **Summersdale Publishers**, on Twitter at
@Summersdale and on Instagram at **@summersdalebooks**
and get in touch. We'd love to hear from you!

Thanks very much for buying this Summersdale book.

www.summersdale.com

IMAGE CREDITS